Tell Me Your

Life Story

MUM

A Mum's Guided Journal and Memory Keepsake Book

What is you full name, birthdate and where were you born?
Share the story behind your name

_____

_____

_____

_____

_____

_____

_____

_____

_____

_____

_____

_____

_____

_____

_____

_____

_____

_____

_____

_____

What was your nickname growing up?
Who gave your childhood nickname?
Do people still call you that today?

Share the story of how and when your parents married.

When and where did your parents get engaged? How old were they?

_____

_____

_____

_____

_____

_____

_____

_____

_____

_____

_____

_____

_____

_____

_____

_____

_____

_____

_____

Share your favorite photo of your parents
at their wedding.

Did your parents have a honeymoon?
Where did they go?

_____

_____

_____

_____

_____

_____

_____

_____

_____

_____

_____

_____

_____

_____

_____

_____

_____

_____

_____

Share a story you've heard about your mother/father's name.
What did you call your father/mother?

Did your father/mother have a nickname? What did his/her siblings or parents call him/her?

Where was your father/mother born?
Where did he/she grow up?

Share your favorite memory of your Dad and Mom..

_____

_____

_____

_____

_____

_____

_____

_____

_____

_____

_____

_____

_____

_____

_____

_____

_____

_____

_____

Name your siblings oldest to youngest. Where do you fit in?

Which sibling were you closest too when growing up?
Which sibling are you closest to today?

Share your favorite photo of you with your siblings.

Share your favorite memory about each of your siblings.

_____
_____
_____
_____
_____
_____
_____
_____
_____
_____
_____
_____
_____
_____
_____
_____
_____
_____
_____
_____
_____
_____
_____

Did you know your Mom and Dad's parents? Share your favorite memory of your grandparents.

_____
_____
_____
_____
_____
_____
_____
_____
_____
_____
_____
_____
_____
_____
_____
_____
_____
_____
_____
_____

Where and when did they get married? Share a story that you've heard about their wedding day.

_____

_____

_____

_____

_____

_____

_____

_____

_____

_____

_____

_____

_____

_____

_____

_____

_____

_____

_____

_____

_____

Share a favorite photo of
your grandparents.

Did your grandparent serve in any war? Which one and where were they located?

Were they awarded any medals or military honors for their service?

_____
_____
_____
_____
_____
_____
_____
_____
_____
_____
_____
_____
_____
_____
_____
_____
_____
_____
_____

Where did he/she die?
How old were you?

Do you have a favorite Aunt or Uncle?
What is their name?

Share your most memorable moments with your Aunts and Uncles.

_____

_____

_____

_____

_____

_____

_____

_____

_____

_____

_____

_____

_____

_____

_____

_____

_____

_____

_____

_____

_____

_____

Who was the better cook, your mom or dad?

_____
_____
_____
_____
_____
_____
_____
_____
_____
_____
_____
_____
_____
_____
_____
_____
_____
_____
_____
_____
_____

What were birthday and holiday celebrations like growing up?
Which holiday was your favorite?

_____

_____

_____

_____

_____

_____

_____

_____

_____

_____

_____

_____

_____

_____

_____

_____

_____

_____

_____

_____

What time of year did your family go on vacation?
Where did your family go on vacation?

Which was the first film you saw at a cinema or drive-in? Who was with you?

_____

_____

_____

_____

_____

_____

_____

_____

_____

_____

_____

_____

_____

_____

_____

_____

_____

_____

_____

_____

_____

Do you remember the first book you read? What was it?

_____

_____

_____

_____

_____

_____

_____

_____

_____

_____

_____

_____

_____

_____

_____

_____

_____

_____

_____

What story do your mom or older siblings tell about your birth?

_____
_____
_____
_____
_____
_____
_____
_____
_____
_____
_____
_____
_____
_____
_____
_____
_____
_____
_____

Share a photo of you as a baby

Did you have a favorite toy? Who gave it to you? Do you still have it?

_____

_____

_____

_____

_____

_____

_____

_____

_____

_____

_____

_____

_____

_____

_____

_____

_____

_____

Where was your childhood home?
Did you share a room or have one of your own?

What were some of your favorite childhood games?

How did you spend your evenings as a child?

_____

_____

_____

_____

_____

_____

_____

_____

_____

_____

_____

_____

_____

_____

_____

_____

_____

_____

_____

_____

_____

Did you have a childhood bedtime? Do you remember what it was?

_____

_____

_____

_____

_____

_____

_____

_____

_____

_____

_____

_____

_____

_____

_____

_____

_____

_____

_____

Share a favorite memory from your childhood.

_____

_____

_____

_____

_____

_____

_____

_____

_____

_____

_____

_____

_____

_____

_____

_____

_____

_____

_____

Share a photo of you as a child.

What type of music did you listen to growing up?
Who was your favorite singer or band?
Did you ever see them perform live?

Which was the first concert that you went too? When and where was that?

_____

_____

_____

_____

_____

_____

_____

_____

_____

_____

_____

_____

_____

_____

_____

_____

_____

_____

_____

In high school, how did you typically spend evenings and weekends?

_____

_____

_____

_____

_____

_____

_____

_____

_____

_____

_____

_____

_____

_____

_____

_____

_____

_____

As a teenager, did you have a curfew? What was it?

_____

_____

_____

_____

_____

_____

_____

_____

_____

_____

_____

_____

_____

_____

_____

_____

_____

_____

_____

When did you learn to drive?
How old were you when you got your license?

_____

_____

_____

_____

_____

_____

_____

_____

_____

_____

_____

_____

_____

_____

_____

_____

_____

_____

_____

_____

What was your first car?
Is there a photo?

_____

_____

_____

_____

_____

_____

_____

_____

_____

_____

first car

What did you wear on your first ever day of school? Is there a photo?

What do you remember about your last ever day of school? Is there a photo?

_____

_____

_____

_____

_____

_____

_____

_____

_____

_____

Name all of the schools that you attended. Which school was your favorite?

What is the most memorable thing about your school years?

_____

_____

_____

_____

_____

_____

_____

_____

_____

_____

_____

_____

_____

_____

_____

_____

_____

_____

What was your greatest achievement during your school years?

_____

_____

_____

_____

_____

_____

_____

_____

_____

_____

_____

_____

_____

_____

_____

_____

_____

_____

_____

_____

Are you still friends with anyone you knew in school? Have any story?

_____

_____

_____

_____

_____

_____

_____

_____

_____

_____

_____

_____

_____

_____

_____

_____

_____

_____

_____

Which university or college did you attend? What did you study at university or college?

_____

_____

_____

_____

_____

_____

_____

_____

_____

_____

_____

_____

_____

_____

_____

_____

_____

_____

Have you done additional study since leaving college/university? What did you study?

How did you get to primary/secondary school every day?

Which year did you start primary/secondary school? How old were during your first year of primary/secondary school?

_____
_____
_____
_____
_____
_____
_____
_____
_____
_____
_____
_____
_____
_____
_____
_____
_____
_____
_____
_____
_____
_____
_____

What were your favorite subjects?
Who were your favorite teachers?

Who was your best friend in primary/secondary school? Are you still friends today?

_____

_____

_____

_____

_____

_____

_____

_____

_____

_____

_____

_____

_____

_____

_____

_____

_____

_____

_____

_____

When you were a kid, what did you want to be when you grew up? Did it happen?

_____

_____

_____

_____

_____

_____

_____

_____

_____

_____

_____

_____

_____

_____

_____

_____

_____

_____

_____

_____

_____

How many places have you worked? Which was your favorite place to work?

_____

_____

_____

_____

_____

_____

_____

_____

_____

_____

_____

_____

_____

_____

_____

_____

_____

_____

_____

Are you or have you been self-employed/had your own business? What was the business?

Are you still friends with anyone you met through any of your jobs or business?

_____

_____

_____

_____

_____

_____

_____

_____

_____

_____

_____

_____

_____

_____

_____

_____

_____

_____

_____

Where was your first job?
What was your role there?

How old were you when you started working? Do you remember how much you were paid?

_____

_____

_____

_____

_____

_____

_____

_____

_____

_____

_____

_____

_____

_____

_____

_____

_____

_____

_____

_____

How long did you stay at that first job? What do you remember the most about that job?

_____
_____
_____
_____
_____
_____
_____
_____
_____
_____
_____
_____
_____
_____
_____
_____
_____
_____
_____
_____

Share a favorite memory from each job you've had during your working life.

_____

_____

_____

_____

_____

_____

_____

_____

_____

_____

_____

_____

_____

_____

_____

_____

_____

_____

_____

_____

What volunteer positions have you held? Why did you choose those organizations?

_____

_____

_____

_____

_____

_____

_____

_____

_____

_____

_____

_____

_____

_____

_____

_____

_____

_____

_____

How did volunteering make you feel? Share about something your volunteer work.

Did you serve in the military?
Which service?

_____

_____

_____

_____

_____

_____

_____

_____

_____

_____

_____

_____

_____

_____

_____

_____

_____

_____

_____

_____

What years did you serve?
What rank did you achieve?

Share a favorite photo

Share your favorite memory from your military service.

_____

_____

_____

_____

_____

_____

_____

_____

_____

_____

_____

_____

_____

_____

_____

_____

_____

_____

_____

_____

_____

How did you meet people?

What is the funniest story you have from your dating life?

How old were you the first time you went on a date? What was their name?

Did they meet your parents before you went out?

_____

_____

_____

_____

_____

_____

_____

_____

_____

_____

_____

_____

_____

_____

_____

_____

_____

_____

_____

_____

_____

Where did you go on that date? Were you nervous?

_____

_____

_____

_____

_____

_____

_____

_____

_____

_____

_____

_____

_____

_____

_____

_____

_____

_____

_____

How did you meet your spouse/significant other?

_____

_____

_____

_____

_____

_____

_____

_____

_____

_____

_____

_____

_____

_____

_____

_____

_____

_____

Do you have pet names/terms of endearment for each other? What are they?

What did you do for your first date? When and where did you get engaged?

Share your favorite memory about finding your first family home.

How many children do you have? What are their names? List them in order of oldest to youngest.

_____

_____

_____

_____

_____

_____

_____

_____

_____

_____

_____

_____

_____

_____

_____

_____

_____

_____

_____

_____

Why those names?
Share the story behind each name.

Do any of them share a room with a sibling? Who shares with who?

_____

_____

_____

_____

_____

_____

_____

_____

_____

_____

_____

_____

_____

_____

_____

_____

_____

_____

_____

Where was they born?

Where about did they grow up?

Share your favorite story of your son and daughter.

_____
_____
_____
_____
_____
_____
_____
_____
_____
_____
_____
_____
_____
_____
_____
_____
_____
_____
_____
_____
_____
_____

How old were you when you got your first passport? Which country was the first stamp in your passport?

How many countries have you spent time in? Have you ever been on a cruise? Where did go?

Do you prefer hotels, caravans or camping?

Have you ever traveled by yourself or always with others?

_____

_____

_____

_____

_____

_____

_____

_____

_____

_____

_____

_____

_____

_____

_____

_____

_____

_____

_____

_____

_____

_____

Which places have been your favorite to visit? Which place were your least favorite to visit?

_____

_____

_____

_____

_____

_____

_____

_____

_____

_____

_____

_____

_____

_____

_____

_____

_____

_____

_____

_____

_____

_____

Share a favorite memory from your travels..

_____

_____

_____

_____

_____

_____

_____

_____

_____

_____

_____

_____

_____

_____

_____

_____

_____

_____

_____

_____

_____

_____

_____

_____

Share a photo your favorite place.

Share a story about the worst experience you had while traveling?

Have you ever been a part of an audience for a TV show? Which show?

Where you a member of the local library growing up or throughout your life?

_____

_____

_____

_____

_____

_____

_____

_____

_____

_____

_____

_____

_____

_____

_____

_____

_____

_____

_____

_____

_____

_____

_____

Do you have a favorite book? What is it? Who are some of your other favorite authors or books?

Did you ever have a crush on a movie star or musician? Who was it? What are some of your other favorite films

Was there a favorite pet? Share a favorite memory about one of your pets.

Name your hobbies?

Share a story about what you remember about each event.

_____

_____

_____

_____

_____

_____

_____

_____

_____

_____

_____

_____

_____

_____

_____

_____

_____

_____

_____

_____

_____

Have you ever had your photo in the newspaper? What was it for?

Are there any tasks you need to complete before you die?

What is most difficult about leaving your loved ones behind?

What is on your bucket list

What do you thing the world needs more of right now?

_____
_____
_____
_____
_____
_____
_____
_____
_____
_____
_____
_____
_____
_____
_____
_____
_____
_____
_____
_____
_____

What do you believe people want the most in life?

_____
_____
_____
_____
_____
_____
_____
_____
_____
_____
_____
_____
_____
_____
_____
_____
_____
_____
_____
_____
_____

What brings you the greatest sense of comfort and peace?

What are you most proud of in life?

Is there any advice you'd like to give us?

_____

_____

_____

_____

_____

_____

_____

_____

_____

_____

_____

_____

_____

_____

_____

_____

_____

_____

_____

_____

What message would you like to share with your family?

_____
_____
_____
_____
_____
_____
_____
_____
_____
_____
_____
_____
_____
_____
_____
_____
_____
_____
_____
_____
_____
_____

Share a family photo

Share a photo

Made in the USA
Las Vegas, NV
07 May 2022

48583478R00066